ANIMAL SAFARI

Leopards

by Megan Borgert-Spaniol

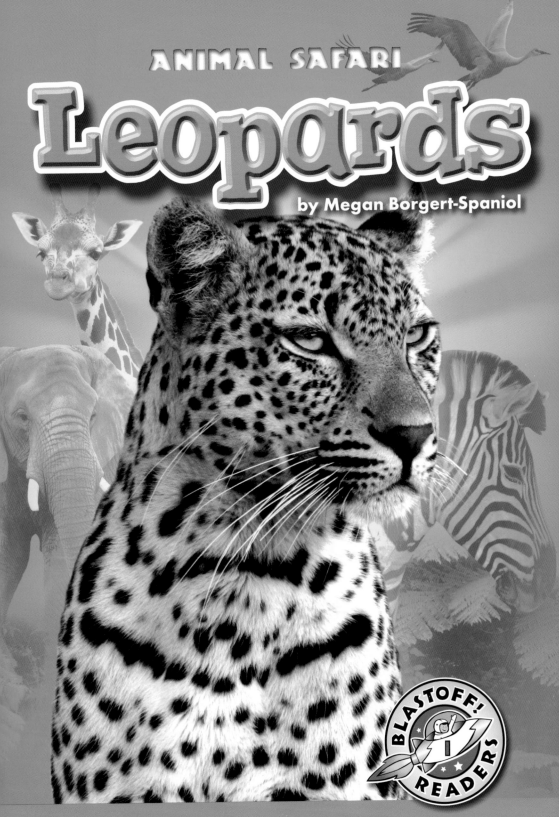

BLASTOFF! READERS

BELLWETHER MEDIA · MINNEAPOLIS, MN

Note to Librarians, Teachers, and Parents:

Blastoff! Readers are carefully developed by literacy experts and combine standards-based content with developmentally appropriate text.

Level 1 provides the most support through repetition of high-frequency words, light text, predictable sentence patterns, and strong visual support.

Level 2 offers early readers a bit more challenge through varied simple sentences, increased text load, and less repetition of high-frequency words.

Level 3 advances early-fluent readers toward fluency through increased text and concept load, less reliance on visuals, longer sentences, and more literary language.

Level 4 builds reading stamina by providing more text per page, increased use of punctuation, greater variation in sentence patterns, and increasingly challenging vocabulary.

Level 5 encourages children to move from "learning to read" to "reading to learn" by providing even more text, varied writing styles, and less familiar topics.

Whichever book is right for your reader, Blastoff! Readers are the perfect books to build confidence and encourage a love of reading that will last a lifetime!

This edition first published in 2013 by Bellwether Media, Inc.

No part of this publication may be reproduced in whole or in part without written permission of the publisher. For information regarding permission, write to Bellwether Media, Inc., Attention: Permissions Department, 5357 Penn Avenue South, Minneapolis, MN 55419.

Library of Congress Cataloging-in-Publication Data
Borgert-Spaniol, Megan, 1989-
  Leopards / by Megan Borgert-Spaniol.
    p. cm. – (Blastoff! readers: animal safari)
  Includes bibliographical references and index.
  Summary: "Developed by literacy experts for students in kindergarten through grade three, this book introduces leopards to young readers through leveled text and related photos"–Provided by publisher.
  ISBN 978-1-60014-769-2 (hardcover : alk. paper)
  1. Leopard–Juvenile literature. I. Title.
  QL737.C23B669 2013
  599.75'54–dc23   2011053020

Printed in the United States of America, North Mankato, MN.

Contents

What Are Leopards?

Leopards are **big cats**. Most have tan coats with dark spots. The spots are called **rosettes**.

Some leopards
have dark coats.
They are called
black panthers.

Where Leopards Live

Leopards live in forests, **deserts**, mountains, and grasslands.

Most leopards live alone. They rest in trees or thick **brush** during the day.

Hunting

Leopards hunt at night. They **stalk** warthogs, antelopes, and baboons.

Sometimes leopards hunt from trees. They hide in the branches and wait to **pounce**.

Leopards drag
their kill into trees.
They must keep their
food away from
lions and hyenas.

Cubs

A female leopard gives birth to two or three **cubs**. They live with her for two years.

Cubs stalk and chase one another. This makes them strong hunters. Good pounce, cub!

Glossary

big cats—large wild cats; lions, tigers, and leopards are all big cats.

brush—thick bushes and plants that cover the ground

cubs—young leopards; cubs live with their mother until they can hunt alone.

deserts—dry lands with little rain; very few plants and animals live in deserts.

pounce—to leap on top of something

rosettes—spots on a leopard's coat; rosettes are shaped like roses.

stalk—to secretly follow

To Learn More

AT THE LIBRARY

Knutson, Barbara. *Sungura and Leopard: A Swahili Trickster Tale.* Minneapolis, Minn.: First Avenue Editions, 2007.

Nussbaum, Ben. *Loli the Leopard.* Norwalk, Conn.: Soundprints, 2006.

Walden, Katherine. *Leopards of the African Plains.* New York, N.Y.: PowerKids Press, 2009.

ON THE WEB

Learning more about leopards is as easy as 1, 2, 3.

1. Go to www.factsurfer.com.

2. Enter "leopards" into the search box.

3. Click the "Surf" button and you will see a list of related Web sites.

With factsurfer.com, finding more information is just a click away.

Index